Content

How to Use This Book

The goal of *Language Development: Grammar and Usage* is to increase the learners' proficiency in language arts skills. The subject matter used in these activities has been chosen based on age appropriateness and the current curriculum being used in schools. The subject matter used in these activities is based on a broad sampling of science and social studies curriculum from across the country. The activities and skills that they test follow a sampling of the National Council of Teachers of English (NCTE) standards. The activities have been designed to capture the learners' interests by presenting material in a fun and exciting way.

Language Development: Grammar and Usage is organized into six sections: Spelling, Sentences, Punctuation, Definitions, Parts of Speech, and Capitalization. Each section focuses on an important aspect of grammar and usage, offering easy-to-understand skill definitions and activity directions.

Spelling

Learners will find themselves challenged by activities that will help them master irregular verbs, irregular plurals, and compound words.

Sentences

The activities in this section help the learner hone his or her skills at constructing proper sentences. Learners will analyze run-on sentences and sentence fragments, gaining an understanding of questions and the importance of proper word order.

2

Punctuation

This section focuses on the importance of punctuation for clear communication. Learners come to understand the correct way to use commas in a series and in addresses. They also learn how to use periods and quotation marks.

Definitions

Learners will use this section to gain knowledge of the importance of defining words. Fun activities include using definitions to solve a crossword puzzle, which entertain learners while educating them about the importance of understanding the meanings of words.

Parts of Speech

This section focuses on two of the most important parts of speech: nouns and verbs. Activities here help learners develop an understanding of the proper functions of nouns and verbs. These activities utilize filling in the blanks and completing charts, making the learning process interactive.

Capitalization

In this final section, learners are given activities to strengthen their understanding of capitalization and its importance in clear written communication.

Name _____

Irregular Verbs

*Verbs are words that show action. To show action that happened in the past, most verbs add **d** or **ed** at the end. Irregular verbs are words that use different endings or even change their spelling to tell about an action that has happened in the past.*
Examples: *take-took, ring-rang, drive-drove*

Directions: Read the following paragraph about bullfrogs. Circle the present-tense irregular verbs. Then match the verbs to their past-tense versions in the list below. Use the box of irregular verbs and their present-tense versions to complete the activity.

Bullfrogs

Bullfrogs are the largest frogs in North America. They can grow to be as large as 8 inches (20 cm) long. Bullfrogs have large mouths. Bullfrogs eat almost any animal smaller than itself.

Present tense	Past tense
grow	ate
eat	had
have	grew

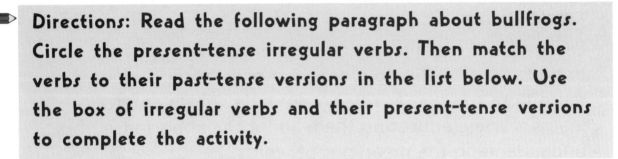

4

Name _____

Run-on Sentences

A run-on sentence is two sentences joined together without any punctuation. Run-on sentences also do not have a word that joins the two sentences together. Some words used to join two sentences together are: and, but, or because.
Example: *Run-on: The dog barked it was hungry.*
          Correct sentence: The dog barked because it was hungry.

Directions: On a separate sheet of paper, rewrite the following run-on sentences using joining words.

Grasshopper Facts

1 Grasshoppers have six legs they use all of them for walking.

2 Most grasshoppers have two pairs of wings some have only one pair.

3 Grasshoppers can jump more than 100 times their length they have strong leg muscles.

4 Grasshoppers eat plants some eat insects, too.

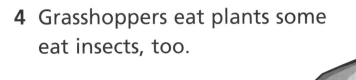

5

Name _____

Periods

Periods are punctuation marks that end statement sentences.
Example: *I like playing soccer.*

Directions: Read the paragraph about motorcycles. Place a period wherever one is needed.

Early Motorcycles

The first motorcycle was invented in 1885. Early motorcycles were bicycles with engines The engines were attached to the bicycles Over the years bicycles improved. Strong bodies and thick tires were used Springs were put on motorcycles to make the ride easier.

Using Definitions to Complete Sentences

Knowing and understanding the definitions of words in a paragraph can help you answer questions about the text or complete sentences using those words.
Example: *Lava is melted rock.*

> **Directions: Read the following text about deserts. Complete the sentences that follow.**

Deserts

Deserts are dry and often sandy areas where hardly any plants grow because there is so little rain. Most deserts are covered with sand. Sand is tiny grains of rock. The rest of the desert land is made up of things such as gravel-covered plains. Plains are large treeless areas.

1 A dry and often sandy area where hardly any

   plants grow is called a _____.

2 Tiny grains of rock are called _____.

3 Large treeless areas are called _____.

Name _____

Fill in the Noun

Nouns are words that name a person, place, or thing.
Example: *I go home. ("Home" is the noun. It names a place.)*

> **Directions: Place each noun where it belongs in the paragraph that follows.**

stores	men	helmets	boots

Firefighters

Firefighters keep our communities safe. Firefighters battle fires

that start in homes, _____, and other places. Both

_____ and women work as firefighters. Firefighters are

members of fire departments. Firefighters use many different

tools to fight fires. They ride in fire trucks. Firefighters

wear clothing that keeps them safe.

They wear _____,

gloves, coats, pants,

and _____.

8

Name _____

First Words

The first word in a sentence always begins with a capital letter.
Example: *It snowed on Monday.*

> **Directions: On a separate sheet of paper, rewrite the sentences so that they are correct.**

Spider Facts

1 spiders have no bones.

2 most spiders are black, brown, or gray.

3 spiders have eight legs.

4 each leg has tiny hairs on it.

5 spiders use these hairs to smell and touch things.

9

Background

• Giving learners the skills and tools to recognize new words, decipher these words, and to identify if a word is spelled correctly, is important to development as readers and writers. Using topics chosen from different content areas, such as science, helps to broaden the learner's knowledge and comprehension.

Homework Helper

• Pull out five words from the Dinosaurs passage (p.12) and write them out. Intentionally misspell three of them. Ask the learner to identify the misspelled word and to spell each one correctly. Then have the learner check spellings using a dictionary.

Research-based Activity

• Have learners do library or Internet research to further their understanding of good nutrition (p. 13). Then have them make a list of all the new words they come across.

Test Prep

• The following activities reflect a broad sampling of state standards. By familiarizing learners with common testing formats, they become more comfortable with district or state spelling tests.

Different Audiences

• To challenge an accelerated learner, try adding another step or question to the activities presented in this section. For example, to improve competency with spelling Irregular Plurals (p. 11) and Irregular Verbs (p. 12), have the learner read through a newspaper or magazine and list the irregular forms that they find. Then they can write their own sentences using these new words.

Name _____

Identifying Irregular Plurals

*To show more than one of something, many words add **s** or **es** at the end. Irregular plurals are words that use other endings or change their spelling to show more than one.*

Examples: wolf   wolves
                baby   babies

> Directions: Read the following list of words. Put an "I" next to the words that are irregular plurals.

1 dishes___

2 knives___

3 books___

4 candies___

5 boxes___

6 leaves___

Challenge: Read through your favorite book. Make a list of all the irregular plurals you find.

Name _____

Dinosaurs

*Verbs are words that show action. To show action that happened in the past, most verbs add **d** or **ed** at the end. Irregular verbs are words that use different endings or even change their spelling to tell about an action that has happened in the past.*

Examples: *Verb ending in d: Present tense: smile Past tense: smiled*
              Irregular Verb: Present tense: drive Past tense: drove

Directions: Read the following paragraph about dinosaurs. Circle the past-tense irregular verbs. Then match them to their present-tense versions. Use the box of irregular verbs and their present-tense versions to complete the activity.

Present tense	Past tense
feed	grew
eat	tore
are	fed
tear	were
grow	ate

Dinosaurs are a group of very large animals who lived on Earth millions of years ago. Dinosaurs were different sizes. Scientists believe some dinosaurs grew to be as long as 130 feet (40 meters). These dinosaurs weighed as much as 85 tons (77 metric tons). Some dinosaurs only fed on plants. Other dinosaurs ate meat. They tore up their food with their sharp teeth.

Name _____

A Good Breakfast Is Important

A compound word is made up of two separate words that are put together to make a new single word.
Example: *dog + house = doghouse*

> **Directions: Use the compound words in the box to complete the following sentences.**

Breakfast	blueberries	pancakes
oatmeal	doughnuts	

_____ is a very important meal to eat. Having a good

breakfast will give you the energy you need to do well in

school. Many people enjoy cold cereal or hot _____. People

may also eat fresh fruit such as bananas or _____. Some

people like to put syrup on their _____. However,

you should not eat foods such as _____

for breakfast. They have too much

sugar and fat in them.

Challenge: Think of three compound words that are not used here.

Name _____

Making Compound Words

A compound word is made up of two separate words that are put together to make a new single word.
Example: *clown + fish = clownfish*

Directions: Draw a line between the words in Column A and the words in Column B to make new words.

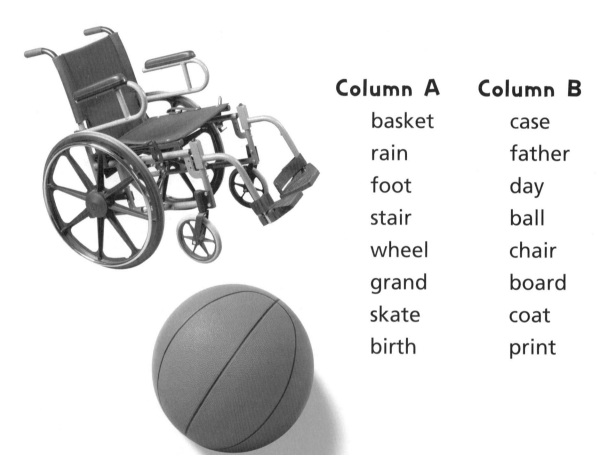

Column A	Column B
basket	case
rain	father
foot	day
stair	ball
wheel	chair
grand	board
skate	coat
birth	print

Challenge: Write a story using the compound words used here.

14

Name _____

Skill Check—Spelling

Irregular Plurals

✏️ **Directions:** Read the following list of words. Put an "I" next to the words that are irregular plurals.

1 cats_____

2 calves_____

3 wishes_____

4 teeth_____

Compound Words

✏️ **Directions:** Use the words in the box to complete the following sentences.

peanut   oatmeal

Healthy Afternoon Snacks

Eating healthy every day is important. After school you

might be hungry. Avoid snacks such as candy bars

or potato chips. Eat foods such as a _____ butter

sandwich or a bowl of _____.

Teaching Tips...

TEACHING TIPS

Background

- It is important for learners to be able to differentiate a correctly punctuated complete sentence from a run-on sentence or sentence fragment. The ability to determine whether a sentence is a statement or a question is also imperative, as is whether or not the words composing the sentence are in proper order. The ability to determine if a sentence is correct or not will aid the learner in not only writing, but reading and speaking.

Homework Helper

- Have a conversation with the learner. Ask the learner a question and have him or her respond with a statement. Then have the learner write down the conversation. Ask them to add a question mark or period to the sentences where appropriate.

Research-based Activity

- Have the learner do Internet or library research to increase his or her knowledge about Early Boats (p. 19) or Earth Day (p. 20). Ask the learner to take brief outline-style notes. Then have the learner write complete sentences, avoiding run-ons.

Test Prep

- State standards were sampled when devising the following activities. Testing often requires learners to demonstrate an understanding of strategies to interpret, comprehend, and evaluate texts similar to the ones found in this section.

Different Audiences

- When dealing with a learner who is on an accelerated learning track, you might want to add a second step to one or more of the activities. This will help challenge the learner and ultimately broaden his or her skills. For example, in the Sentence Fragments activity (p. 18), after the learner has completed the activity, write out several more fragments and have the learner turn them into complete sentences.

Name _____

Earthworms

A run-on sentence is two sentences joined together without any punctuation. Run-on sentences also do not have a word that joins the two sentences together. Some words used to join two sentences together are: and, but, or because.

Example: *Run-on: The dog barked it was hungry.*

Correct sentence: The dog barked because it was hungry.

Directions: On a separate sheet of paper, rewrite the following run-on sentences using joining words.

1 Earthworms' bodies look smooth they are also shiny.

2 You can barely see some earthworms they are so small.

3 Earthworms cannot see they can sense light.

4 Earthworms like cool, dark places they do not like the heat and sun at all.

Challenge: Read over any essay or report you have written. See if there are any run-on sentences. If there are, rewrite the sentences using joining words.

Name _____

Plane Facts

A fragment is a group of words that do not contain a complete thought. A sentence fragment is missing either a subject or a verb. Remember that all complete sentences have a subject and a verb.
Examples: *No subject: parked the car*
Correct Sentence: She parked the car.

Directions: Turn these sentence fragments into complete sentences. Choose from the subjects and verbs in the box below.

Wright Brothers	It	flown

1 The _____
built the first plane.

2 _____ flew 120 feet.

3 In 1939, the first jet plane was

_____.

Challenge: Look at the movie ads in the newspaper. Circle all the ads that use sentence fragments, such as "...best ever..." to sell a movie.

18

Name _____

Early Boats

Questions are sentences that ask something. A question starts with a capital letter and has a question mark (?) at the end of the sentence. Statements are sentences that state a fact.
Examples: *Question: How are you?*
Statement: I am happy.

Directions: Read the following sentences and put a question mark at the end of the sentences that are asking a question. Put a period at the end of sentences that state a fact.

1 How long have people been using boats _____

2 People have been using boats for thousands of years _____

3 What were some of the first boats ever made _____

4 Dugout canoes were some of the first boats _____

5 How are dugout canoes made _____

6 Dugout canoes were made by burning out

the inside of a log _____

Challenge: At dinner, listen to your family talk. Write down some of the questions the people in your family ask one another. Before you do this, ask your family if you can write what they say.

19

Name _____

Earth Day

The words in a sentence need to be in the right order to make sense.
Example: *Wrong Order: late for school am I*
    Correct Sentence: I am late for school.

Directions: Rewrite the following sentences. Make sure that the words are in the right order. Then capitalize the first word in the sentence and add a period at the end of the sentence.

1 was held in 1970 the first Earth Day

_____

2 remind people of the need to care for our planet it was held to

_____

3 become a problem pollution and littering had

_____

4 celebrate Earth Day people all over the world

_____

5 April 22 every year since 1990, Earth Day has been held on

_____

Name _____

Skill Check—Sentences

Fragments

Directions: Turn these sentence fragments into complete sentences. Choose from the subjects and verbs in the box below.

| trains | used | burned |

1 The first _____ were built in the 1820s.

2 Some trains _____ steam engines.

3 Wood or coal was _____ to make the steam.

Word Order

Directions: Rewrite the following sentences. Make sure the words are in the right order. Then capitalize the first word in the sentence and add a period at the end of the sentence.

1 is a day for Arbor Day planting trees

_____

2 started in Nebraska in 1872 Arbor Day was

_____

21

Teaching Tips...

Background

• Giving learners the abilities and tools to identify and apply proper punctuation will strengthen their communication skills in the areas of reading, writing, and speaking. Additionally, by sampling topics across the curriculum, learners' comprehension in areas such as social studies and science is greatly improved.

Homework Helper

• Have learners write out sentences that require the use of commas. For example, ask the learner to write a sentence about his or her favorite foods, activities, or sports. Learners can also make a list of important dates in history, making sure that commas are used in the correct manner.

Research-based Activity

• Have learner do the activity on page 26. Ask him or her to ask more questions about Thanksgiving. Then have the learner do research at a library or on the Internet to answer their questions in writing, with proper use of question marks, commas, and periods.

Test Prep

• State standards were used in the formulation of the following activities. Common standardized tests require learners to be able to read a unit of text and be able to respond to it during tests given by the state. The activities that follow give learners experience in this testing format.

Different Audiences

• When working with accelerated learners, activities should be expanded so that learners are challenged. For example, in the Quotation Marks activity (p. 26), have the learner add to the written conversation, by writing new dialogue about Thanksgiving, using quotation marks appropriately.

The Ocean Biome

Commas are punctuation marks used to set off words in a series.
Example: *For lunch we ate soup, sandwiches, French fries,
and bananas.*

> **Directions: Read the paragraph about the ocean biome.
> Then place commas where they are needed in the
> facts following the paragraph.**

Our planet is made up of different kinds of ecological communities. These ecological communities are called biomes. Grasslands, deserts, and oceans are examples of biomes. Below you will find some facts about the ocean biome.

1 The ocean supplies us with food energy and minerals.

2 The ocean floor has valleys plains mountains and even volcanoes.

3 Fish squid plankton and whales are just some of the beings that live in the ocean.

Challenge: Read a newspaper or magazine to see the many ways that commas are used.

Name _____

Thomas Alva Edison

Commas are used in addresses and dates to break up a series of information. Using commas makes it easier to understand the information being given.
Examples: *He lives in Los Angeles, California.*
She was born on December 29, 1999.

Directions: Read the paragraph about Edison. Then place commas where they are needed in the addresses and dates that follow.

Thomas Alva Edison was a great inventor. He invented many things that made life better for people. He invented early forms of the record player, movie camera, and lightbulb. Here are some other facts about Edison.

1 Thomas Alva Edison was born on February 11 1847.

2 When he was a boy, he lived in Milan Ohio.

3 In 1876, he built a lab in Menlo Park New Jersey.

4 Thomas Alva Edison died on October 18 1931.

Now write out your birthday and address. Remember to put the commas where they belong.

5 I was born on _____.

6 I live in _____.

Name _____

Early Bicycles

Periods are punctuation marks that end statement sentences.
Example: *I like playing baseball.*

> **Directions: Read the paragraph about bicycles.**
> **Add periods to the sentences that need them.**

The first bicycle was built around 1817. It was mostly made of wood Early bicycles did not have pedals Instead, riders sat on the seat and walked or ran with the bicycle The first bicycles with pedals were made around 1866.

Challenge: Write down some questions. Then rewrite them so that they are statements. Remember to use periods.

25

Name _____

The First Thanksgiving

Quotation marks are used to show the exact words a person says. Quotation marks are placed before the person's first word and after their last word, following the punctuation mark that ends the sentence.
Example: *Karen said, "Let's go shopping."*

Directions: Place quotation marks where they are needed in the following conversation about the first Thanksgiving.

1 Adam said, The first Thanksgiving was held in the fall of 1621 in Plymouth, Massachusetts.

2 Joan replied, It was attended by the Pilgrims and the Wampanoag Indians.

3 Adam said, The Pilgrims were honoring their first harvest in America.

4 Maria smiled and said, Over one hundred and forty people came to the party.

5 Joan said, Everyone ate, danced, and played games.

6 Maria said, That first Thanksgiving lasted three days.

Challenge: The next time you are watching television, write down some of the things the people say. Then add quotation marks where they are needed.

26

Name _____

Skill Check—Punctuation

Using Commas in Addresses and Dates

✏️ **Directions: Place commas where they are needed in the following sentences.**

Eli Whitney

1 Eli Whitney was born in Westborough Massachusetts.

2 He was born on December 8 1765.

3 Whitney invented the cotton gin.

4 The cotton gin removed seeds from cotton.

5 Eli Whitney died on January 8 1825.

Quotation Marks

✏️ **Directions: Place quotation marks where they are needed in the following conversation about Flag Day.**

Flag Day

1 Adam said, Flag Day is held every year on June 14.

2 Joan replied, It was started to honor the American flag.

3 Adam said, On Flag Day people display the flag on their homes.

4 Joan added, The flag is also flown at businesses and other public places.

Teaching Tips...

Background

• Giving learners tools to decode and apply the definitions of words will support their developing communication skills in reading, writing, and speaking. Working across the curriculum helps learners improve comprehension and vocabulary in several content areas, such as science.

Homework Helper

• Have learners pull five words that are unfamiliar to them from a fiction story. Ask them to write a definition for each word based on the words in the surrounding text or context. Then have them look up the words in a dictionary to see how well their definitions match up.

Research-based Activity

• Using information from the Volcanoes (p. 30) or Trees (p. 32) passages, have learners draw and label a picture of a volcano or tree, including definitions with the labels. They should do additional library or Internet research to select the specific kind of tree or volcano they will draw and label.

Test Prep

• The following activities are based on a sampling of state standards. While filling in the blanks remains a standard testing format, learners increasingly need to be able to read a block of text and respond to it on state tests. The following activities give learners practice in both.

Different Audiences

• If you are working with an accelerated learner, try adding a second step to each activity to further challenge the child. For example, after using the crossword puzzle activity on page 29, have learners write sentences using the words they used to complete the puzzle.

TEACHING TIPS

28

The Space Shuttle

A definition is an explanation of what a word or phrase means.
Example: *Word: Agree Definition: To say yes to something.*

Directions: Read the following definitions. Choose the word it defines from the box. Write the word in the crossword puzzle.

space shuttle astronaut cargo launch mission orbiter

1 a spacecraft that carries people and cargo between Earth and space. (2 words)

2 a person who travels into space

3 to move quickly off the ground

4 an errand or task that people are sent somewhere to do

5 supplies carried by the space shuttle

6 the part of the space shuttle that goes back and forth between Earth and space

Name _____

Volcanoes

Knowing and understanding the definitions of words in a paragraph can help you answer questions about the text or complete sentences using those words.

✏️➡ **Directions: Read the following paragraph about volcanoes. Then complete the sentences that follow.**

A volcano is a mountain with openings. The mouth of the volcano is called the crater. The crater is located at the top of the volcano. Volcanoes give off lava. Lava is melted rock. The melted rock comes from the inside of the volcano. The lava is very hot. When volcanoes give off lava, it is called an eruption.

1 A mountain with openings is called a _____.

2 The mouth of the volcano is called the _____.

3 The melted rock a volcano gives off is called _____.

4 When a volcano gives off lava it is called an _____.

Challenge: There are different kinds of volcanoes. Do some library or Internet research to find definitions for different kinds of volcanoes.

Name ______________________________

Using Definitions in Labeling

Butterflies

In order to label the parts of something, you must know what it is. Understanding the definition of something can help you label it.

Directions: Read the following paragraph about butterflies. Then label the parts of the butterfly on the picture below using words from the box below.

head	feelers	body	wings	legs

The body of a butterfly has three main parts. The first part is the head. The head has the butterfly's eyes, mouth, and feelers. The feelers are thin and long. They are used to smell, hear, and touch. The second part of the butterfly is where the wings and legs are attached. A butterfly has two pairs of wings. It has a front pair of wings and a back pair of wings. Butterflies have six legs. The third part of the butterfly's body holds the important body parts inside it.

1 ______________________

2 ______________________

3 ______________________

4 ______________________

5 ______________________

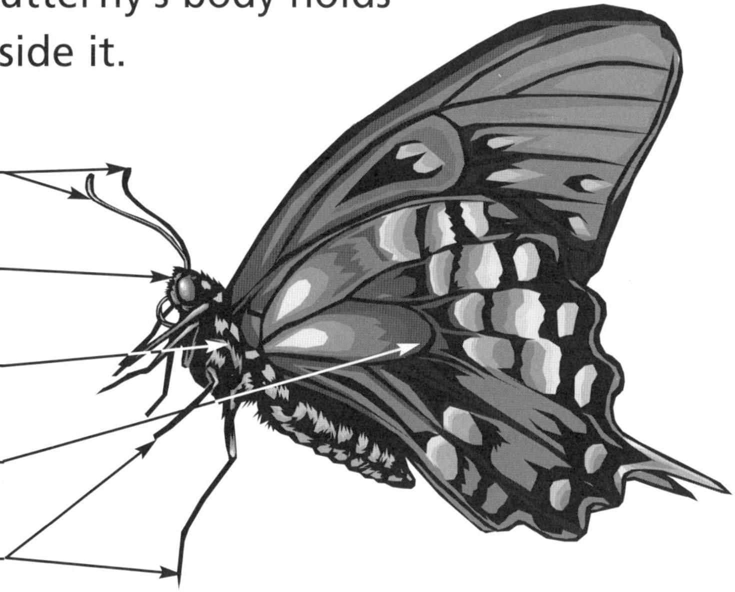

Name _____

Trees

Remember, a definition explains what a word means.
To use a word correctly, you need to know its definition.

**Directions: Read the following paragraph about trees.
Then, in the list below, draw a line from the part of
the tree to what it does.**

Trees have three main parts. Trees have roots, a trunk with branches, and leaves. The roots are at the bottom of the tree. Roots grow under the ground. They help keep the tree standing. The trunk and branches are like the body and arms of the tree. The leaves of a tree grow out of the branches. Leaves turn sunlight into food for trees.

Leaves   These grow under the ground.

Trunk   These turn sunlight into food.

Branches   Leaves grow out of them.

Roots   The body of a tree.

Challenge: Make a list of five different kinds of trees. Write a definition for each tree which explains what is special about that kind of tree.

Name _____

Skill Check—Definitions

Using Definitions to Complete Sentences

> Directions: Read the paragraph about caves.
> Then complete the sentences that follow.

Caves

Caves are large holes that are underground or in the side of a hill. Many caves have thin pieces of rock that hang from their roofs. These thin pieces of rock look like icicles. The hanging pieces of rock are called stalactites.

1 Large holes that are underground or in the sides of a hill are

called _____.

2 Thin pieces of rock that hang from the roof of a cave are

called _____.

Using Definitions in Labeling

> Directions: Label the parts of the bat using the
> following words: ears, eyes, wing.

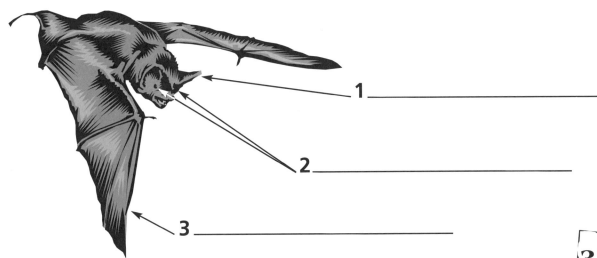

1 _____

2 _____

3 _____

Background

• Providing learners with the tools needed to understand sentence syntax, with an emphasis on the proper use of nouns and verbs will help them develop strong communication skills in reading, writing, and speaking. Additionally, reading a variety of curriculum-related texts will improve learners' understanding and knowledge in different content areas, such as social studies.

Homework Helper

• Have learners read a chapter from their favorite book. Then have them list all the nouns and verbs in the chapter they have read. Next, have the learner write new sentences using the nouns and verbs they listed.

Research-based Activity

• Using the Police Officers passage (p. 36) as a starting point, have the learners do more in-depth research about police officers, either at a library or on the Internet. Have them list all the nouns and verbs pertaining to police officers and their work.

Test Prep

• Understanding language conventions such as parts of speech is a common testing area of state standards. The nonfiction passages in this section further assist the learner in interpreting and evaluating texts, another expectation of state standards.

Different Audiences

• It is very important to challenge the learner, especially one that is an accelerated learner. Adding extra questions or new steps to the activities will help reinforce the learner's comprehension for these particular skill sets.

Name _____

All About Banks

Nouns are words that name a person, place, thing, or animal.
Example: *My brother has a dog. (The word "brother" names*
a person. The word "dog" names an animal.)

Directions: Read the following paragraph. Circle the nouns. Then, in the chart below, write the nouns you circled, telling whether they name a person, place, or thing. Some nouns appear more than once. You only need to write down the first time they appear.

Banks are places where people keep their money and other valuables. The bank you see in your community is a branch of a banking company. Many people keep their money in a bank. They put their money into an account. An account helps you keep track of how much money you have. The people you see behind the long counters at the bank are called tellers. They help customers add money to their account or take it out.

People	Places	Things

35

Name _____

Police Officers

Nouns are words that name a person, place, thing, or animal.
Example: *I go to school. ("School" names a place.)*

Directions: Place each noun where it belongs in the paragraph that follows.

crime	car	patrol officer
detective	criminals	communities
police academy	jobs	law

Police officers keep our _____ safe. They make sure

people follow the _____. All police officers must

study for about six months at a _____. They learn

how to drive a _____ in a high-speed chase. They also

learn how to arrest _____. After their training,

there are many different _____ a police officer can

have. A _____ walks or drives through a com-

munity. He or she is looking to make sure no one is breaking

the law or needs help. A _____ is an officer who

tries to figure out who committed a _____.

Doctors Without Borders

Verbs are words that show action. Verbs show or tell what a person or a thing is doing.
Example: *The boys run around. ("Run" tells what the boys are doing.)*

> **Directions: Read the paragraph below. Circle the verb in each sentence.**

Doctors Without Borders is a group of doctors and nurses. These medical people travel all over the world. They work in more than 80 countries. Many of the places they go do not have any doctors. They bring medicine with them. Doctors Without Borders helps many people who are sick or hurt. The doctors give the medicine to the sick people. The medicine makes the sick people feel better. Doctors Without Borders helps millions of people every year.

Challenge: Write your own story about a doctor helping someone. Use the verbs you circled in the Doctors Without Borders paragraph.

37

Name _____

The Statue of Liberty

Verbs are words that show action. Verbs show or tell what a person or a thing is doing.
Example: *The girls jump rope. ("Jump" tells what the girls are doing.)*

> **Directions: Place each verb where it belongs in the paragraph that follows.**

put	stands	holds	visit

The Statue of Liberty is one of the largest statues ever made.

It was made in France. France gave the statue to America

in 1886. The statue was _____ on an island near New

York City. The statue holds a tablet in its left hand. In its right

hand, the statue _____ a torch. The statue

_____ for America's freedom. Many people

_____ the Statue of Liberty each year.

Challenge:
Using these same verbs,
write a composition
about another important
American statue or building.

Name _____

Skill Check—Parts of Speech

Nouns

➡ **Directions: Read the following text. Circle the nouns and write them in the correct column.**

Schools

Children go to school. Teachers help children learn. Teachers write lessons on blackboards. Students write notes in their notebooks.

Person	Place	Thing

Fill in the Verb

➡ **Directions: Place each verb where it belongs in the paragraph that follows.**

has	cut	finish	visit

Mount Rushmore

Mount Rushmore _____ the faces of four presidents on it.

The four faces _____ into Mount Rushmore are George Washington, Thomas Jefferson, Abraham Lincoln, and Theodore Roosevelt.

It took about 14 years to _____ Mount Rushmore.

About two million people _____ Mount Rushmore every year.

39

Background

- To develop good communication skills in reading, writing, and speaking, learners need to have the proper tools to understand and apply capitalization whenever it is called for. By working across different areas of the curriculum, learners improve their comprehension and vocabulary in different content areas. They also get examples of the proper use of capitalization that reinforces what they learn from the activities.

Homework Helper

- Have learners write about their day at school. They should use capital "I" in narrating their story.

Research-based Activity

- Using the Bald Eagle passage (p. 43) as a starting point, have learners research the topic further, either at the library or on the Internet. Then have them write out five more statements about bald eagles. Be sure that they follow proper capitalization rules.

Test Prep

- The activities that follow are based on a variety of state standards. Filling in the blanks remains a standard testing format. However, now more than ever, learners need to be able to read blocks of text and then answer questions about it on state tests.

Different Audiences

- If you are dealing with a special education learner, you may want to focus on only one or two of the questions posed in any one activity. For example, in the Alexander Graham Bell activity (p. 41), have the learner do only two or three parts of the activity instead of all six. Then if the learner does well, you can move on to the next part of the activity.

Name _____

Alexander Graham Bell

The names of people and places always start with capital letters.
Examples: *Name of Person: George Washington*
Name of Place: Boston, Massachusetts

> **Directions: Circle the names of a person or place in each sentence.**

1 Alexander Graham Bell was an inventor.

2 He was born in Scotland.

3 His family moved to the United States.

4 Bell invented the telephone in March 1876.

5 He formed the Bell Telephone Company in 1877.

6 Bell won a prize from France for his work.

Challenge: With a parent or relative, write out the names and addresses of people in your family. Then tape these addresses to a map that shows the states where they live.

Name _____

White House

The names of people and places always start with capital letters.
Example: *The White House is located at 1600 Pennsylvania Avenue in Washington, D.C.*

Directions: Read the postcard. Underline the words that need to be capitalized.

Dear aunt edna,

Today in school we learned about the white house. President John adams was the first president to live in the White House. He moved in around 1800. The White House has 132 rooms.

Love, jane

Edna Smith

22 Gibson Drive

Ridgefield, New Jersey 00000

Name _____

Bald Eagle

The first word in a sentence always begins with a capital letter.
Example: *Today it will rain.*

Directions: The first word in a sentence always begins with a capital letter. On a separate sheet of paper, rewrite the sentences so that they are correct.

1 the bald eagle is the national bird of the United States.

2 it is called "bald" because it has white feathers on its head.

3 bald eagles use sticks to make nests on top of tall trees.

4 they live near bodies of water, such as lakes or streams.

5 fish, snakes, and crabs are some of the animals that bald eagles hunt for food.

Challenge: With a friend, write down sentences without the first word capitalized. Then take turns correcting each sentence.

43

Park Cleanup

The word "I" is always capitalized.
Example: *My friend Anna and I went to the movies.*

Directions: Read the paragraph about cleaning up a park. Circle all the places that need to have the capital "I."

My classmates and i want to help keep our community clean. We go to the community park to pick up garbage. i wear gloves to keep my hands clean. i pick up bottles, cans, and papers. i put the bottles and cans in one bag. i put the papers in another bag. We take the bottles, cans, and papers to a recycling center. There they will be reused and made into new things. My classmates and i like to help our community.

Challenge: Write a report about anything you have done in or out of school. Remember to use the word "I" to tell your story.

Name _____

Skill Check—Capitalization

Names of People and Places

> ✏️ **Directions:** Circle the name of a person or place in each sentence.

1 Granville Woods was an inventor.

2 He was born in Columbus, Ohio.

3 He was born on April 23, 1856.

4 As a young man he moved to New York City.

5 In 1887, Woods invented a machine that made traveling by train safer.

First Words

> ✏️ **Directions:** The first word in a sentence always begins with a capital letter. On a separate sheet of paper, rewrite the sentences so that they are correct.

The Cardinal

1 the cardinal is a bird found in many parts of the United States.

2 cardinals are mostly red in color.

3 a female cardinal usually lays three or four eggs.

4 among the things cardinals eat are seeds, wild fruit, and beetles.

Answer Key

p. 4
grow - grew
eat - ate
have - had

p. 5
1) Grasshoppers have six legs **and** they use all of them for walking.
2) Most grasshoppers have two pairs of wings **but** some have only one pair.
3) Grasshoppers can jump more than 100 times their length **because** they have strong leg muscles.
4) Grasshoppers eat plants **and** some eat insects, too.

p. 6
The first motorcycle was invented in 1885. Early motorcycles were bicycles with engines (.) The engines were attached to the bicycles (.) Over the years bicycles improved. Strong bodies and thick tires were used (.) Springs were put on motorcycles to make the ride more comfortable.

p. 7
1) desert
2) sand
3) plains

p. 8
Firefighters keep our communities safe. Firefighters battle fires that start in homes, **stores**, and other places. Both **men** and women work as firefighters. Firefighters are members of fire departments. Firefighters use many different things to fight fires. They ride in fire trucks. Firefighters wear clothing that keeps them safe. They wear **helmets**, gloves, coats, pants, and **boots**.

p. 9
1) Spiders have no bones.
2) Most spiders are black, brown, or gray.
3) Spiders have eight legs.
4) Each leg has tiny hairs on it.
5) Spiders use these hairs to smell and touch things.

p. 11
1) dishes
2) knives I
3) books
4) candies I
5) boxes
6) leaves I

p. 12
Dinosaurs are a group of very large animals who lived on Earth millions of years ago. Dinosaurs **were** different sizes. Scientists believe some dinosaurs **grew** to be as long as 130 feet (40 meters). These dinosaurs weighed as much as 85 tons (77 metric tons). Some dinosaurs only **fed** on plants. Other dinosaurs **ate** meat. They **tore** up their food with their sharp teeth.

p.13
Breakfast is a very important meal to eat. Having a good breakfast will give you the energy you need to do well in school. Many people enjoy cold cereal or hot **oatmeal**. People may also eat fresh fruit such as bananas or **blueberries**. Some people like to put syrup on their **pancakes**. However, you should not eat foods such as **doughnuts** for breakfast. They have too much sugar and fat in them.

p. 14
basketball, raincoat, footprint, staircase, wheelchair, grandfather, skateboard, birthday

p. 15
Irregular Plurals
1) cats
2) calves I
3) wishes
4) teeth I

Compound Words
Eating healthy every day is important. After school you might be hungry. Avoid snacks such as candy bars or potato chips. Eat foods such as a **peanut** butter sandwich or a bowl of **oatmeal**.

p. 17
1) Earthworms' bodies look smooth **and** they are also shiny.
2) You can barely see some earthworms **because** they are so small.
3) Earthworms cannot see **but** they can sense light.
4) Earthworms like cool, dark places **and** they do not like the heat and sun at all.

p. 18
1) Wright Brothers
2) It
3) flown

p. 19
1) How long have people been using boats(?)
2) People have been using boats for thousands of years(.)
3) What were some of the first boats ever made(?)
4) Dugout canoes were some of the first boats(.)
5) How are dugout canoes made(?)
6) Dugout canoes were made by burning out the inside of a log(.)

p. 20
More than one correct answer is possible
1) The first Earth Day was held in 1970.
2) It was held to remind people of

the need to care for our planet.

3) Pollution and littering had become a problem.

4) People all over the world celebrate Earth Day.

5) Since 1990, Earth Day is held on April 22 every year.

p. 21
Fragments
1) The first **trains** were built in the 1820s.

2) Some trains **used** steam engines.

3) Wood or coal was **burned** to make the steam.

Word Order
More than one correct answer is possible
1) Arbor Day is a day for planting trees.

2) Arbor Day was started in Nebraska on April 10, 1872.

p. 23
1) The ocean supplies us with food(,) energy(,) and minerals.

2) The ocean floor has valleys(,) plains(,) mountains(,) and even volcanoes.

3) Fish(,) squid(,) plankton(,) and whales are just some of the living beings that live in the ocean.

p. 24
1) Thomas Alva Edison was born

February 11(,) 1847.

2) When he was a boy, he lived in Milan(,) Ohio.

3) In 1876, he built a lab in Menlo Park(,) New Jersey.

4) Thomas Alva Edison died on October 18(,)1931.

5) More than one correct answer is possible

6) More than one correct answer is possible

p. 25
The first bicycle was built around 1817. It was mostly made of wood(.) Early bicycles did not have pedals(.) Instead, riders sat on the seat and walked or ran with the bicycle(.) The first bicycles with pedals were made around 1866.

p. 26
1) Adam said, (")The first Thanksgiving was held in the fall of 1621 in Plymouth, Massachusetts.(")

2) Joan replied, (")It was attended by the Pilgrims and the Wampanoag Indians.(")

3) Adam said, (")The Pilgrims were honoring their first harvest in America.(")

4) Maria smiled and said, (")Over one hundred and forty people came to the party.(")

5) Joan said, (")Everyone ate, danced, and played games.(")

6) Maria said, (")That first Thanksgiving lasted three days.(")

p. 27
Using Commas in Addresses and Dates
1) Eli Whitney was born in Westborough(,) Massachusetts.

2) He was born on December 8(,) 1765.

3) Whitney invented the cotton gin.

4) The cotton gin removed seeds from cotton.

5) Eli Whitney died on January 8(,) 1825.

Quotation Marks
1) Adam said, (")Flag Day is held every year on June 14.(")

2) Joan replied, (")It was started to honor the American flag.(")

3) Adam said, (")On Flag Day people display the flag on their homes.(")

4) Joan added, (")The flag is also flown at businesses and other public places.(")

p. 29
1) space shuttle
2) astronaut
3) launch
4) mission
5) cargo
6) orbiter

p. 30
1) volcano
2) crater
3) lava
4) eruption

p. 31
1) feelers
2) head
3) body
4) wings
5) legs

p. 32
1) Leaves
   These turn sunlight into food.

2) Trunk
   The body of a tree.

3) Branches
   Leaves grow out of them.

4) Roots
   These grow under the ground.

p. 33
Using Definitions to Complete Sentences
1) caves

2) stalactites

Using Definitions in Labeling
1) ears
2) eyes
3) wing

p. 35
People
people
tellers
customers

Places
banks
bank
community
branch
company

Things
money
valuables
account
counters

47

. 36

Police officers keep our **communities** safe. They make sure people follow the **law**. All police officers must spend about six months at a **police academy**. They learn how to drive a **car** in a high-speed chase. They also learn how to arrest **criminals**. After their training, there are many different **jobs** a police officer can have. A **patrol officer** walks or drives through a community. He or she is looking to make sure no one is breaking the law or needs help. A **detective** is an officer who tries to figure out who committed a **crime**.

p. 37

Doctors Without Borders **is** a group of doctors and nurses. These medical people **travel** all over the world. They **work** in more than 80 countries. Many of the places they **go** do not **have** any doctors. They **bring** medicine with them. Doctors Without Borders **helps** many people who **are** sick or hurt. The doctors **give** the medicine to the sick people. The medicine **makes** the sick people **feel** better. Doctors Without Borders **helps** millions of people every year.

p. 38

The Statue of Liberty is one of the largest statues ever made. It was made in France. France gave the statue to America in 1886. The statue was **put** on an island near New York City. The statue holds a tablet in its left hand. In its right hand, the statue **holds** a torch. The statue **stands** for America's freedom. Many people **visit** the Statue of Liberty each year.

p. 39
Parts of Speech
Nouns

Person
teachers
children
students

Place
school

Thing
blackboards
lessons
notebooks
notes

Fill in the Verb
Mount Rushmore **has** the faces of four presidents on it.

The four faces **cut** into Mount Rushmore are George Washington, Thomas Jefferson, Abraham Lincoln, and Theodore Roosevelt.

It took about 14 years to **finish** Mount Rushmore.

About two million people **visit** Mount Rushmore every year.

p. 41
1) Alexander Graham Bell
2) Scotland
3) United States
4) Bell
5) Bell Telephone Company
6) Bell, France

p. 42
Dear **Aunt Edna**,

Today in school we learned about the **White House**. President John **Adams** was the first president to live in the White House. He moved in around 1800. The White House has 132 rooms.

Love, **Jane**

p. 43
1) **The** bald eagle is the national bird of the United States.

2) **It** is called "bald" because it has white feathers on its head.

3) **Bald** eagles use sticks to make nests on top of tall trees.

4) **They** live near bodies of water, such as lakes or streams.

5) **Fish**, snakes, and crabs are some of the animals that bald eagles hunt for food.

p. 44
My classmates and **I** want to help keep our community clean. We go to the community park to pick up garbage. **I** wear gloves to keep my hands clean. **I** pick up bottles, cans, and papers. **I** put the bottles and cans in one bag. **I** put the papers in another bag. We take the bottles, cans, and papers to a recycling center. There they will be reused and made into new things. My classmates and **I** like to help our community.

p. 45
Names of People and Places
1) Granville Woods
2) Columbus, Ohio
3) April
4) New York City
5) Woods

First Words
More than one correct answer is possible

1) **The** cardinal is a bird found in many parts of the United States.

2) **Cardinals** are mostly red in color

3) **A** female cardinal usually lays three or four eggs.

4) **Among** the things cardinals eat are seeds, wild fruit, and beetles.

© Rosen School Supply•Brain Builders Grammar and Usage•2•RSS